W9-AYI-154

EDGE BOOKS™

FULL THROTTLE

MONSTER TRUCKS

by
Jeff Savage

Consultant:
Ralph Moore
President
Edge-Motorsports

CAPSTONE PRESS
a capstone imprint

Edge Books are published by Capstone Press,
151 Good Counsel Drive, P.O. Box 669, Mankato, Minnesota 56002.
www.capstonepress.com

Printed in the United States of America in Stevens Point, Wisconsin.
062011
006228WZVMI

 Books published by Capstone Press are manufactured with paper
containing at least 10 percent post-consumer waste.

Library of Congress Cataloging-in-Publication Data
Savage, Jeff, 1961–
    Monster trucks / by Jeff Savage.
    p. cm. — (Edge books. Full throttle)
    Includes bibliographical references and index.
    Summary: "Describes the first monster trucks, how monster trucks are built,
and their performances in shows"— Provided by publisher.
    ISBN 978-1-4296-3943-9 (library binding)
    1. Monster trucks — United States — Juvenile literature. 2. Truck racing —
United States — Juvenile literature. I. Title. II. Series.
GV1034.996.S37 2010
796.7 — dc22   2009022118

Editorial Credits
Carrie Braulick Sheely, editor; Tracy Davies, designer; Jo Miller, media researcher;
    Laura Manthe, production designer

Photo Credits
Alamy/Michael Doolittle, 22; Alamy/PCN Black, 17, 18, 20; AP Images/
Bloomsburg Press Enterprise/Bill Hughes, 15; AP Images/Carol Francavilla, 11;
AP Images/Mike Derer, 26; Art Life Images/BIGFOOT4x4, 8, 10; Art Life
Images/Huntoon-Action Images, cover, 12, 14, 27 (top), 28, 29; CORBIS/
Transtock/Winston Luzier, 27 (bottom); Newscom, 5, 7, 19, 23; Newscom/Icon
SMI/Imago/Fishing 4, 24; Newscom/Icon SMI/Imago/Pius Koller, 13

Artistic Effects
Dreamstime/In-finity; Dreamstime/Michaelkovachev; iStockphoto/Michael Irwin;
iStockphoto/Russell Tate; Shutterstock/Els Jooren; Shutterstock/Fedorov Oleksiy;
Shutterstock/jgl247; Shutterstock/Marilyn Volan; Shutterstock/Pocike

Table of Contents

More than 40,000 fans filled the Alamodome on January 11, 2009, in San Antonio, Texas. They expected a Monster Jam show filled with heart-pounding action.

All eyes were on the monster truck El Toro Loco. Driver Lupe Soza was from Orange Grove, Texas, a town near San Antonio. He wanted to put on a good show for his hometown fans. The night before, Soza had come close to winning the **freestyle** event. Could he earn the win today?

The course was tough. In fact, there had never been so many obstacles set up before in San Antonio.

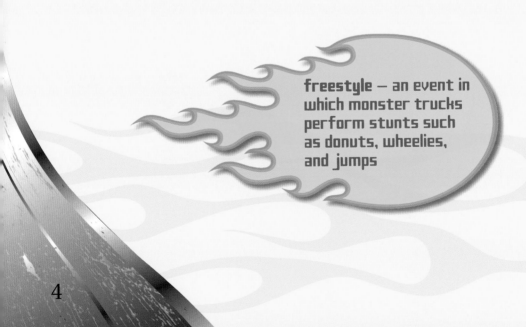

freestyle — an event in which monster trucks perform stunts such as donuts, wheelies, and jumps

This row of junked cars was just one obstacle Soza faced on January 11, 2009.

Fast Fact: The vehicles that monster trucks crush are borrowed from local junkyards. They are returned after the shows.

When it was Soza's time to shine, he stomped on the throttle. It looked like his run was going well. Then El Toro Loco launched over a double obstacle that included two buses and several junked cars. The truck landed with a thud and nearly tipped over on its side! But Soza's experience behind the wheel helped him make an amazing save. Before his time was up, Soza had made not one, but two saves to keep his 10,000-pound (4,536-kilogram) truck grounded. With a score of 30, he beat Damon Bradshaw in the U.S. Air Force Afterburner, who had earned 29 points.

The crowd roared with excitement. Not only had Soza won the freestyle event, but he had edged out Superman for the win in racing. By winning both events, he earned the Double Down award.

Fast Fact: In 2004, Lupe Soza, Tom Meents, and Debrah Miceli all won the freestyle event at the Monster Jam World Finals. The event ended in a three-way tie.

Soza waved to the crowd after winning the racing event in San Antonio.

RISE OF THE MONSTERS

Today's most popular monster trucks are household names. But this wasn't always the case. Just 40 years ago, there was no such thing as a monster truck.

Bob Chandler faced challenges like this steep hill head-on with Bigfoot.

THE FIRST MONSTER

In the early 1970s, four-wheel-drive pickups were becoming popular. In these trucks, the engine powers all four wheels. Four-wheel-drive helps keep vehicles from slipping on icy or loose surfaces.

In 1974, Bob Chandler opened a parts supply store for four-wheel-drive trucks in Hazelwood, Missouri. To advertise, Bob put several **custom** parts on his 1974 F-250 pickup and drove it around town. With its 48-inch (122-centimeter) tires, Bob's truck stood out.

Bob drove his truck hard. He often broke engine parts. Bob was told that he had a "big foot" that pressed too hard on the throttle. Bob then decided to name his truck Bigfoot.

custom — describes a part that is specially made; custom parts aren't part of a vehicle's original design from the factory.

9

The original Bigfoot was so popular that Bob built another Bigfoot in 1982. **Promoters** often asked Bob to show off Bigfoot 2 at truck and tractor pulls. One 1983 appearance went especially well. At this event, Bob drove Bigfoot 2 into the middle of the Pontiac Silverdome in Michigan. The crowd watched curiously as the truck rumbled up to a row of junked cars. Chandler revved the engine. Bigfoot 2 rolled up onto the cars, crushing them like toys.

The crowd roared. Fans poured onto the field to surround the truck and take pictures. The promoters sat back and smiled. They knew it was only a matter of time before more monster trucks took center stage at shows.

Bigfoot trucks weren't the feature of early shows, but they got a lot of attention.

promoter — a person or company that puts on a sporting event, such as a monster truck show

MONSTER MADNESS GROWS

The promoters were right. It seemed like monster trucks popped up almost overnight. Bear Foot was one of Bigfoot 2's first competitors. Fred Shafer had built this monster truck from a Chevrolet pickup in 1979. With 66-inch (168-centimeter) tires, the two trucks were evenly matched. They faced off in car-crushing competitions throughout the early 1980s.

In 1984, nearly 72,000 fans filled the Silverdome to see Bigfoot and Bear Foot, along with other monsters. The massive trucks took turns crushing rows of junked cars.

Bear Foot shows off its awesome car-crushing power at a public stunt in 1990.

Fast Fact: Model numbers aren't shown on Bigfoot trucks. To fans, each truck is known only as "Bigfoot."

11

MORE THAN CAR CRUSHING

Fans couldn't get enough of the sights and sounds of crunching metal. Yet they longed for even more excitement. They wanted to know which truck could travel the fastest and soar the highest.

In 1986, the first monster truck race was held at the Astrodome in Houston, Texas. Soon afterward, promoters created shows that included high-flying stunts off ramps.

The speed of side-by-side racing was a hit with fans.

Today, about 300 monster trucks compete in shows around the United States. Among the most popular trucks are Grave Digger, Bigfoot, Maximum Destruction, and Raminator. Grave Digger's popularity led the crew to create seven different models. These trucks often appear in shows the same night in different cities.

There are also 16 Bigfoots. Six are race trucks. Five of these racers compete in the United States, and one races in Europe. Many of the others are display trucks that often appear at public events.

Some monster trucks stand out from the others. Batman looks like the Batmobile from the comic book. Superman is a giant Ford F-150 with a long red "cape," and Monster Mutt looks like a dog!

Chad Fortune has been tearing up the Monster Jam scene in Superman since 2005.

13

Although they were popular, the first monster trucks were heavy, slow-moving beasts. Over time, though, improvements turned monster trucks into lightweight speed machines. Modern trucks soar and spin like acrobats on wheels. They rocket off ramps, reaching heights of at least 15 feet (4.6 meters).

To perform these amazing stunts, a monster truck is built for top performance. Monster trucks use auto racing parts, tractor parts, and sometimes even parts from forklifts or school buses.

Most builders follow safety rules set by the Monster Truck Racing Association (MTRA). The MTRA approves trucks that meet its design requirements.

Monster trucks regularly soar more than 80 feet (24 meters) in length.

Monster trucks are best known for their giant tires. The largest tire size allowed for nearly all competitions is 66 inches (168 centimeters) high and 43 inches (109 centimeters) wide. Each tire weighs about 500 pounds (227 kilograms).

In the early days, monster trucks used tires made for farming equipment. Today, Firestone and other tire companies make tires just for monster trucks.

Instead of completely filling tires with air, crews keep the tire pressure low. This feature helps create softer, bouncier landings after jumps. The tires can flatten almost completely when landing.

Monster truck tires have large bumps called treads for better grip on loose surfaces.

The huge tires on monster trucks are one of their most noticeable features. But roaring engines are another feature almost impossible to ignore. Monster trucks use powerful engines made for drag racing cars. The engine is mounted behind the driver. Most engines are 575 cubic inches (9,423 cubic centimeters) in size. A standard pickup engine is about two-thirds that size.

A monster truck engine produces about 1,500 horsepower, which is about five times more than a standard pickup. Part of this mega-power comes from using a supercharger. This blower forces extra air into the engine.

A fuel called methanol also helps engines crank out power. But this power does come at a price. The engine burns about 1 gallon (3.8 liters) of fuel every 100 feet (30 meters). At a cost of about $7.00 per gallon, crews have steep fuel bills.

The hard-working engines take a beating at shows. The parts constantly endure bumps and jolts. Running methane fuel is also hard on engines. Crews replace engines often. Some teams burn through five engines in a year!

supercharger

On average, a supercharger increases an engine's horsepower by about 46 percent. But horsepower gains of more than 85 percent are possible.

Fast Fact: Monster truck engines are so loud that many fans wear earplugs at shows.

CHASSIS AND BODY

A frame, or chassis, supports a monster truck. The truck body, engine, and other main parts all connect to the chassis. The chassis is made of strong steel tubes that are welded together. Most truck crews build their own chassis.

The body of a monster truck is made of fiberglass. This material is lighter than steel. Keeping a truck's weight down helps it travel faster and jump higher. Fiberglass is also easier to repair than steel. Some crews own several bodies in different styles. These crews can replace one body with another on the same chassis.

Tube-shaped frames have been common since the early 1990s.

Many crews pay more than $5,000 for custom paint jobs on truck bodies. Painters make the designs using an airbrush. This tool uses air to spray the paint. Painters control how much paint is sprayed with a trigger. Airbrushing is much more accurate than painting with a brush.

Some paint jobs feature cartoon-like characters.

Fast Fact: Some monster truck cab floors are made of a clear material called Plexiglas. Drivers can look through the floor to watch what they are crushing or to see where they are landing.

AXLES AND SUSPENSION SYSTEM

A monster truck's axles come from farm, military, or other large vehicles. They must be strong to withstand more than 4.5 tons (4 metric tons) pressing down on them.

Just like in other four-wheeled vehicles, front and rear suspension systems connect the axles to the frame. On a monster truck, four steel bars connect each axle to the frame for extra strength. Coiled steel shock absorbers are part of each suspension system. They act like giant springs. During a hard landing, the truck bounces instead of landing stiffly.

Suspension systems can provide up to 3 feet (.9 meter) of **wheel travel**. Extra space between the tires and the body allow for this high wheel travel. A standard pickup has only about 10 inches (25 centimeters) of space between its wheels and body.

Grave Digger's red shock absorbers stand out against its green frame.

Monster Trucks at a Glance

Weight:	4.5 to 5 tons (4 to 4.5 metric tons)
Height:	about 12 feet (3.7 meters)
Weight of one tire:	about 500 pounds (227 kilograms)
Maximum tire size:	5.5 feet (1.7 meters) tall, 3.5 feet (1 meter) wide
Cost of each tire:	about $2,600
Body material:	fiberglass
Chassis material:	steel
Chassis width:	12 feet (3.7 meters)
Engine size:	575 cubic inches (9,423 cubic centimeters)
Engine horsepower:	about 1,500; some trucks produce up to 2,000 horsepower.
Engine type:	supercharged V-8
Cost of an engine:	about $35,000
Transmission:	automatic with three or four gears
Fuel type:	methanol
Fuel consumption:	about 100 feet (30 meters) per gallon
Top speed:	about 80 miles (129 kilometers) per hour
Number of competitive monster trucks:	about 300
Cost of a competitive monster truck:	about $180,000

wheel travel — the distance between the highest point the suspension system can move to its lowest point

SAFETY FIRST!

Plenty can go wrong in a monster truck show. In crashes, tires can tear off and engines can catch fire. A driver performing a huge wheelie could lose control and flip over backward.

Because accidents can happen, crews take safety seriously. The driver can push an ignition interrupter switch on the dashboard to stop the engine. Safety officials also hold a remote ignition interrupter (RII) for each truck. They can shut off a truck that appears out of control.

Drivers wear safety gear, and they're also surrounded by it. Each driver wears a helmet, neck restraint, fireproof suit, and gloves. A safety harness straps the driver tightly into the seat. The truck's steel roll cage helps keep the cab from being crushed during rollovers.

Even with safety equipment, drivers do get injured sometimes. The trucks get hurt too. The average show truck has between $2,500 and $5,000 worth of damage each week.

The roll cage surrounds a driver from all sides.

Monster Jam World Finals

The Monster Jam World Finals is one of the biggest monster truck events. This weekend competition happens each spring in Las Vegas, Nevada. Fans fill Sam Boyd Stadium to see the world's top trucks battle in races and freestyle competitions.

In the first World Finals in 2000, Tom Meents won the racing event in the truck Goldberg. Dennis Anderson won the freestyle event in Grave Digger. Meents has won seven championship titles over the years. Anderson is next with three championships to his name.

SHOW ACTION

Monster truck shows bring heart-pounding, ear-numbing action to fans in the United States, Canada, and Europe. Promoters often put on tours. Tours include a series of shows held in various cities. Popular tours include Monster Jam and Monster Nationals. Shows usually feature two main competitions — side-by-side racing and freestyle.

Because trucks have similar designs, drivers must rely on their skill in Monster Jam races.

Most monster truck races are similar to drag races. Two trucks line up next to each other at the starting line. When the green light flashes, the trucks roar toward the finish line. Along the way, drivers may meet rows of junked cars, jumps, water puddles, and hills. The winner is the driver who crosses the finish line first. Racecourses are often set up in a straight line, but they may have a J-shape or an oval layout. Outdoor racecourses are usually longer than indoor courses.

Most races use the bracket format. A bracket is a set of rounds. If eight trucks are competing, there will be four races in the first round. The four winning trucks advance to the second round. The two winning trucks in that round go on to the final round. The driver who wins the final round is the overall winner.

Fast Fact: In 2007, the video game *Monster Jam* was released. Players can "drive" one of 20 trucks that compete in the actual series.

In freestyle contests, each monster truck is given a set amount of time, usually three to five minutes. During this time, the truck is free to perform stunts. Almost any stunt goes. Trucks do wheelies and donuts. They smash junked cars, fly off ramps, and spray dirt into the air.

Winners are determined either by the loudest audience applause or by official judging. With judging, three trackside officials score each performance from 0 to 10. Thirty points is the highest possible score. Drivers Dennis Anderson and Mike Vaters are well-known freestylers.

Some shows have separate wheelie or donut competitions. Like in freestyle, judges score the drivers based on their performances.

While performing sky wheelies, trucks stand nearly vertical.

Sending dirt flying can rack up points in freestyle.

Maximum Destruction sails over a line of buses during a freestyle event in 2006.

If there is a high-energy monster truck race happening, Jim Koehler is probably in the middle of it. Jim's performances are so action-packed that he is known as "Mr. Excitement."

Jim grew up around motorsport racing. He cheered for NASCAR drivers Richard Petty and Dale Earnhardt. As a teenager, he competed in off-road events like mud races. The first time he drove a monster truck, he was hooked.

Today, Jim lives near Detroit, Michigan. His monster truck garage is larger than one-third of a football field. Jim has two main trucks – Wrecking Crew and Avenger. He uses the same frame for both trucks by replacing one body with the other.

Besides racing, Jim performs amazing stunts with his trucks. He won the freestyle event at the 2003 Monster Jam World Finals.

NON-STOP ACTION

For drivers and crews, the monster truck action never stops. Drivers often attend pit parties before competitions. At these gatherings, fans can meet drivers, see trucks up close, and get autographs. After shows, crews load up their trucks and travel to the next event. It's a busy lifestyle, but it's one they truly love. Driver Greg Adams said, "I do this because I like it. When you tear up your trucks . . . you get irritated, because you want them to be perfect. But I like being a monster truck driver."

Rescue crews always stand ready to help drivers after a crash.

Fast Fact: Monster truck teams spend about $250,000 each year maintaining and repairing a truck.

GLOSSARY

axle (AK-suhl) — a rod attached to the middle of a wheel on a vehicle; axles turn the wheels.

chassis (CHA-see) — the frame on which the body of a vehicle is built; the chassis holds together all the other parts of a monster truck.

custom (KUHS-tuhm) — describes a part that is specially made; custom parts do not come on vehicles built at a factory.

fiberglass (FY-buhr-glas) — a strong, lightweight material made from thin threads of glass

freestyle (FREE-styl) — a monster truck event in which trucks perform stunts such as donuts, wheelies, and jumps

horsepower (HORSS-pou-ur) — a unit for measuring an engine's power

off-road (OFF-rohd) — describes a motorsport event in which vehicles travel on unpaved surfaces such as gravel and other natural terrain

promoter (pruh-MOH-tur) — a person or company that puts on a sporting event

suspension system (suh-SPEN-shuhn SISS-tuhm) — the system of springs and shock absorbers that absorbs a vehicle's up-and-down movements

throttle (THROT-uhl) — a foot pedal that controls how much fuel and air flow into an engine; a monster truck driver steps on the throttle to speed up.

wheel travel (WEEL TRAV-uhl) — the distance between the highest point the suspension system can move to its lowest point

READ MORE

Gigliotti, Jim. *Monster Trucks.* Racing Mania. New York: Marshall Cavendish Benchmark, 2010.

Graham, Ian. *Monster Trucks.* Mankato, Minn.: QEB, 2009.

Levete, Sarah. *Monster Trucks.* Mean Machines. Chicago: Raintree, 2005.

O'Hearn, Michael. *The Kids' Guide to Monster Trucks.* Kids' Guides. Mankato, Minn.: Capstone Press, 2010.

INTERNET SITES

FactHound offers a safe, fun way to find Internet sites related to this book. All of the sites on FactHound have been researched by our staff.

Here's all you do:

Visit *www.facthound.com*

FactHound will fetch the best sites for you!

Index